A Brush Full of Colour

The World of Ted Harrison

Margriet Ruurs
& Katherine Gibson

pajamapress

An Ann
Featherstone Book

Hardcover edition first published in the United States in 2015
Hardcover edition first published in Canada in 2014
Paperback edition first published in Canada and the United States in 2021
Text copyright © 2014 Margriet Ruurs
Text copyright © 2014 Katherine Gibson
This edition copyright © 2021 by Pajama Press, Inc.

10 9 8 7 6 5 4 3 2 1

www.pajamapress.ca   info@pajamapress.ca

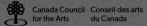 Canada Council   Conseil des arts
for the Arts   du Canada

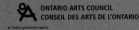 ONTARIO ARTS COUNCIL
CONSEIL DES ARTS DE L'ONTARIO
an Ontario government agency
un organisme du gouvernement de l'Ontario

Canada

The publisher gratefully acknowledges the support of the Canada Council for the Arts and the Ontario Arts Council for its publishing program. We acknowledge the financial support of the Government of Canada through the Canada Book Fund (CBF) for our publishing activities.

Library and Archives Canada Cataloguing in Publication

Ruurs, Margriet, 1952-, author   A brush full of colour : the world of Ted Harrison / Margriet Ruurs & Katherine Gibson.

Includes bibliographical references and index. ISBN 978-1-927485-63-7 (bound) | 978-1-77278-226-4 (softcover)

1. Harrison, Ted, 1926- --Juvenile literature. 2. Painters-- Canada-- Biography--Juvenile literature. 3. Landscape painting, Canadian--Juvenile literature. I. Gibson, Katherine, 1951-, author II. Title.

ND249.H377R88 2014   j759.11   C2014-903711-2

Publisher Cataloging-in-Publication Data (U.S.)

Names: Ruurs, Margriet, author. | Gibson, Katherine, 1951-, author.

Title: A Brush Full of Colour : The World of Ted Harrison / Margriet Ruurs & Katherine Gibson.

Description: Toronto, Ontario Canada : Pajama Press, 2021. | Updated edition. | Includes bibliographic references and index. | Summary: "The story of how a boy's passion for learning saved him from a life in England's coal mines and led him to a career as an internationally acclaimed artist and illustrator, famed for his images of Canada's north. Includes color reproductions of Ted Harrison's art and a preface by the artist"— Provided by publisher.

Identifiers: ISBN 978-1-92748-563-7 (hardcover) | 978-1-77278-226-4 (softcover)

Subjects: LCSH: Harrison, Ted, 1926-2015 – Juvenile literature. | Painters – Canada – Biography – Juvenile literature. | Landscape painting, Canadian – Juvenile literature. | BISAC: JUVENILE NONFICTION / Art / Painting. | JUVENILE NONFICTION / Biography & Autobiography / Art.

Classification: LCC ND249.H33 |DDC 759.11 – dc23

Design by Rebecca Buchanan

Manufactured in China by WKT Company

Pajama Press Inc.
469 Richmond St. E Toronto, ON M5A 1R1

Distributed in Canada by UTP Distribution
5201 Dufferin Street Toronto, Ontario Canada, M3H 5T8

Distributed in the U.S. by Ingram Publisher Services
1 Ingram Blvd., La Vergne, TN 37086, USA

Cover Image: *Magnificent Yukon, 2005; acrylic*
Back Cover: *Northern Education, 1989; acrylic ink serigraph*
Title Page: *Magnificent Yukon (detail), 2005; acrylic*
Back Flap: *Dancing Kites, 1992; acrylic*

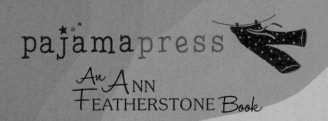
pajamapress
An Ann Featherstone Book

Dancing Kites, 1992; acrylic
Harrison's paintings are full of movement. The kites
and the sky appear to dance together.

To Ted and in fond
memory of Nicky; and
to my Yukon friends—
especially Jan Koepke
—M.R.

To children everywhere,
especially in the Yukon
and County Durham
—K.G.

Storm Lovers, 1992; acrylic ink serigraph
Faceless figures and a crackling sky dominate this painting.
A dashing red rabbit and flying scarf balance the scene.

Contents

'Thirty Below'

Ted Harrison '89.

Victoria B.C.
Dear Readers,

I am pleased to write the foreword to this book, which I hope will introduce many new readers and lovers of art to my life and work. During my career as a teacher, author and artist, I've had the pleasure of meeting students from different parts of the world. Through the years they have influenced my simple artistic style and helped bring my stories and painting to life. If I have inspired them to find their way as artists, I am truly grateful.

I urge you to keep on reading, writing and painting. Develop your own style and keep it honest and true to who you are. Find inspiration in the world around you, and you will make the world a happier and more creative place.

Affectionate regards –
Ted Harrison

Thirty Below, 1984; acrylic ink serigraph
Yukoners enjoy the day, even in the coldest weather.

7

"We should all try to spread a little happiness wherever we may be."

That has been Ted Harrison's life motto. Born and raised in England, Ted has travelled to and lived in many countries. While the scenery and cultures around him changed, one thing stayed the same: his desire to paint. And paint he did. Combining what he learned in art school with the colours and forms he saw around the world, Ted developed his unique style, making him one of Canada's most recognized and popular painters. While telling author Katherine Gibson his life story for her book, *Ted Harrison: Painting Paradise*, Ted chuckled and said, "When people first saw my paintings, some called it folk art. Others just shook their heads and thought I was off my rocker. I call it the School of Cheery!"

Bringing Home the Tree, n.d.; acrylic
Harrison loved to choose whatever colours appealed to him at the time.

Childhood

The Harrison twins as babies, 1926

Edward (Ted) Hardy Harrison and his twin sister Mary Algar (Olga) were born on August 28, 1926, in Wingate, County Durham, England. Wingate was in the heart of England's coal-mining region. Ted wasn't surrounded by colour. The hills were black and the villages were grey. When it rained, everything looked drab, even the hard-working villagers.

Ted's father worked as a coal miner, and later as an insurance salesman. He disliked being down in the mines. Miners worked hard for little pay. The workers went on strike, but the conditions didn't improve very much. Ted's father worked hard to make a living for his family. He vowed that his children would never work in the mines but become educated so they could find a better way of life.

The Harrison home was warm and loving. Ted's mother kept the house clean and the children well dressed. She baked her own bread and cooked rabbit stew and pies for the children. And she often made Ted and Olga's favourite treat: gingerbread men.

The Harrisons were a happy family. In winter, Ted's mother kept the potbelly stove in the small kitchen glowing. They sang by the piano, went sledding and made snowmen with their friends. In summer, the children explored the woods and went fishing.

Olga and Ted, age 3, 1929
Mrs. Harrison was a talented seamstress, so the children were always well dressed.

9

Ted's father liked to sketch and draw in the evenings after work. When Ted was only two, his father gave him a pencil and paper. "Draw!" he said. "I'm sure you will like it as much as I do." He showed his son how lines on paper could make trees, a house, or a hill.

In primary school Ted won his first prize ever. "We had to draw a picture of an apple," he remembers, "and Mrs. Farnworth liked my lovely green apple best of all." She presented him with an award: a framed picture of a sailboat. "That sailboat helped me dream of faraway places."

When Ted grew older, his Latin and English teacher, Mr. Grice, encouraged him to paint. "He told me to draw the nearby walls of Roman ruins," Ted recalls. "And he let me use his private library and map collection." Ted built an "art studio": a hut in the garden. He even painted the inside of the outhouse.

Baby Ted with his father, 1926
Ted often said that he was proud to be a miner's son.

Wingate Colliery in the Snow, 1950; oil ▶
This is one of only a few paintings Harrison made of Wingate. What does it say about the landscape of County Durham? Compare this to "Thirty Below" on pages 6-7. Which painting makes you feel the cold more?

A proper education was important to the Harrisons. Ted's father had quit school at the age of twelve to work in the mines; he never wanted the same life for his son. One day, Ted's parents gave the twins an encyclopedia set. "It was the best gift ever," said Ted. "I read every page of those books and more than once too." He loved to read. After he finished Robert Louis Stevenson's *Treasure Island*, he drew his own treasure map. He devoured books by Jack London: *The Call of The Wild* and *White Fang*. He also read books by the poet Robert Service, about the gold rush and a place far away in northern Canada.

Treasure map, circa 1940; pen and ink
Harrison dreamed of adventures beyond his village. To make the map look hundreds of years old, he used a flame to singe the edges of the paper and added notes in "Olde English."

Ted, circa 1940, with a favourite pet

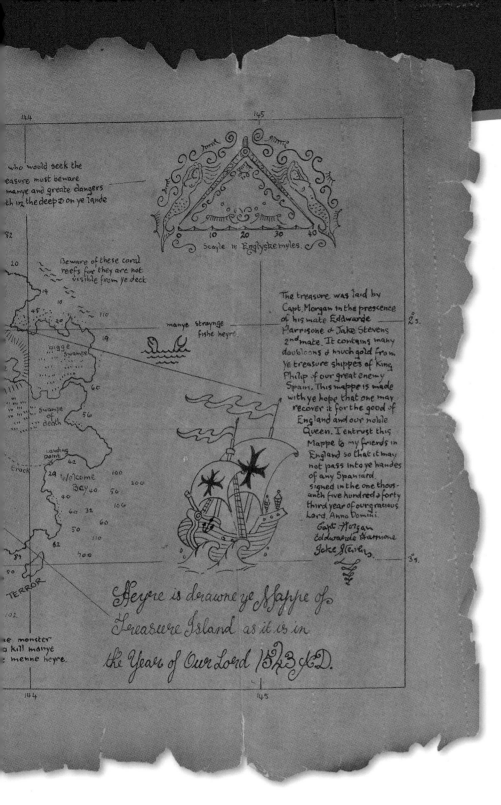

Apple crate label, circa 1930

When Ted was eleven, he started work in his uncle's store packing groceries after school. He used his earnings to go to the cinema, where he saw movies about distant places that captured his imagination.

It was during World War II, when food was scarce, that Ted and Olga saw something they would never forget. A large wooden crate of apples was sent to County Durham from British Columbia, Canada. Ted was given one of the shiny red apples. It was so beautiful that he kept it for days, just to look at it, before sharing it with his family.

Travelling the World

In 1943, when the twins were seventeen, Olga began nurse's training while Ted entered the Hartlepool College of Art. He intended to become a teacher one day. But, like all young men in England during the war, Ted was ready to serve his country as soon as he turned eighteen. He wanted to see the world. It wasn't until the spring of 1946, almost a year after the war ended and after special training in intelligence, that Ted sailed to Bombay, India, on a British military ship. While he was assigned confidential services, Ted took note of India's culture. He drew sketches of exotic fruits, small huts and people dressed in scarves and headdresses.

Next, Ted was assigned military duties in northern Africa, and he landed in Egypt. How different the desert sands were from India! Later, his duties took him to Kenya in East Africa. Crossing the Serengeti Plain, Ted marvelled at the sunlight and the ever-changing colours. He loved Africa, and his sketchbook filled with drawings of the scenery and its people.

After his years of service, he said, "I have seen the

Ted on a motorcycle in Mombasa, Kenya, circa 1947

world and found its many moods—sometimes happy but very often sad. At least, we should all try to spread a little happiness wherever we may be." And he vowed that his paintings would show only positive images. "There's enough sadness and misery in the world without hanging it on our walls."

Impressions of Native Quarter, 1948; watercolour and ink ▶
Harrison believed that subjects for paintings could be found right outside your door. What do you think the painting says about this street in Egypt?

Impressions of Native Quarter Mer...

Travelling the World

Back in England and discharged from the army, Ted became an art teacher. During his holidays he drew and painted as much as he could: zoo animals in Germany, landscapes in Scotland.

One day Ted spotted an advertisement for an art teacher in Malaysia. He jumped at the chance, and he settled quickly into his new position. Ted enjoyed his students and his job. But most of all, he loved the colours of Malaysia: the sunshine, flowers, butterflies, waterfalls and tea plantations—it was nothing like the bleak coal-mining hills of County Durham. He painted colours lit by bright sunlight. He studied the shadows and the many shades of green in the landscape. He continued to sketch people and scenery. He even painted a huge Buddha in a cave: the Perak Tong Temple Buddha, which you can still see today.

While in Malaysia, Ted became best friends with an administrator of the school where he taught. Her name was Nicky and she was from Scotland. On November 12, 1960, they married. Ted and Nicky left Malaysia and moved to New Zealand, where Ted taught for three years. New Zealand was good to them. Ted studied the bold colours and black outlines of Maori art. And best of all, they adopted their son, Charles.

Perak Tong Temple Buddha, 1958; unknown medium; photograph by J.W. Tucker, 1992
The figure in this painting includes details not found in Harrison's later Yukon figures. How are they different?

By 1965, Ted's mother had died, so Ted, Nicky and Charles moved back to England to be closer to his father. But as much as he loved seeing his father and sister again, Ted wasn't happy with his new teaching post at Wingate School. He was expected to follow a strict course of study; he couldn't be creative at all.

Toro Ahua, 1966; acrylic ▶
This painting shows the influence of Maori art. Heavy black outlines also appear in Harrison's early Yukon paintings.

Two years later, and twenty-five years after first reading about a country called Canada in his beloved Jack London books, Ted, Nicky, and Charles moved to Canada to teach in Wabasca, Alberta, 200 miles (322 kilometres) north of the city of Edmonton. "We had no idea just how big Canada was," Ted remarked.

Ted thought it would be easy to emigrate to an English-speaking country. But there were many words in Canada that he did not understand. One day he told Nicky about a stolen cat that was worth $15,000. They were amazed and decided that it must have been a rare breed, maybe a Persian. Later, of course, they learned that the large machines used for building roads in Canada's north were called caterpillars—or "cats" for short.

Untitled, 1967; pen and ink
Harrison loved to fish. What does the clothing say about the people and the climate in which they live?

Ted loved teaching his Cree second graders. They brought him unusual gifts, like a bird's egg or the skull of a muskrat. In return, he told them funny stories and drew pictures for them. He soon discovered that the early readers featuring North American children like *Dick and Jane* had no meaning at all for his Cree and Métis students. So he and another teacher wrote and illustrated a small book filled with northern images instead. Those booklets would be used in the schools for many years.

Ted began to draw and paint new scenes: children playing in snow, log cabins and northern animals.

Untitled illustrations, 1967; pen and crayon
This drawing is a playful depiction of life in northern Alberta.

Ted loved his job in Wabasca, but he still wondered about the Yukon of Robert Service's books. Fellow teachers told him more and encouraged him to apply for a job in Carcross, Yukon. So he did, and he was hired.

The family drove 1,177 miles (1,894 kilometres) north from Wabasca to Carcross. Ted fell in love with the majestic mountains and the clear lakes of the Yukon wilderness. "Carcross looked like a toy town," he recalls.

Ted taught mathematics, reading and science to his elementary students, while Nicky studied to become a kindergarten teacher. She later incorporated kindergarten into the public schools, a first in her area.

When he wasn't teaching, Ted painted along roadsides and in meadows. One day, he drove to a spot overlooking Bennett Lake with Montana Mountain in the background. At first it seemed to go well, as he mixed his colours and applied them to the board on his easel. But soon he was frustrated. The land felt alive to him. There was so much movement, so many colours. How could he paint this sky and these mountains?

Ted realized that his style of painting wouldn't work in the Yukon.

Untitled illustration, 1968; pen and ink

Harrison included this drawing in a letter he sent to his sister in England. He wrote, "The ice crystals from one's breath stick to the edges of the parka." A parka lined in fur? Although it could be bitterly cold in County Durham, no one dressed like they did in the Yukon, so Harrison added labels to describe each piece of clothing.

Mountains Bennett Lake, 1968; acrylic ▶

This is the last painting Harrison made in the style he'd learned at art school. How does it differ from his later paintings of the Yukon?

Ted's art training had been very strict. "My head was full of rules as to what I should and shouldn't do." But his heart yearned to use the free lines of nature around him. The northern lights danced in the sky for him, teasing him with their changing colours and shapes. Snow-capped mountains reflected themselves in crystal clear lakes, daring him to paint their outlines.

"I'm going to paint my Yukon!" he told Nicky. So he did.

◀ *Our Cabin, 1971; acrylic*
A typical day at Ted Harrison's cabin at Crag Lake. What features are missing from the faces of the people? How is this painting similar to "Toro Ahua" on page 17?

Yukon Sky, 1983; acrylic ink serigraph
The northern lights blaze with colour. What do the ravens and the figures tell us about the weather that day?

Moko Lizard, 1966; acrylic
This painting, rendered before Harrison went to Canada, features the three primary colours. Compare his use of colour to "Cowboy Charles."

All of the styles and techniques he had seen around the world—in African art, in Asian temples, in the aboriginal paintings of New Zealand and India—would come together in his Yukon paintings.

Ted painted a portrait of his son, which he called "Cowboy Charles." In the background, he painted lopsided buildings and children playing. Later, "Child of the Midnight Sun" showed more buildings, mountains, the sky and six purple suns. He outlined his figures and buildings in black, and the colours he used were unusual.

Cowboy Charles, 1970; acrylic
Note the size of the people in this early Yukon painting. Why do you think that Harrison made his main character so much bigger than the other figures?

Child of the Midnight Sun, 1971; acrylic
This early Yukon painting is two-dimensional. The original painting is taller and includes a total of six suns. Why do you think he depicted so many suns? How are the colours similar to "Moko Lizard" and "Cowboy Charles" on page 24?

A pink moose? A lopsided house? People did not seem to like it. At his first art show in Whitehorse, no one bought any of his paintings. But on the last day of the show, a visitor from Ottawa bought three of Ted's paintings. "I couldn't believe anyone would actually *pay* for my work," said Ted.

Back in Ottawa, the man displayed the art and invited his friends to see it. One friend, an art collector, invited Ted to give a show there. His art was a hit. People bought his paintings even before the show opened. In 1972, he exhibited in Vancouver, where people lined up to see his work.

Caribou Hotel, 1971; acrylic
Another early Yukon painting. How do these colours compare to Harrison's later Yukon paintings? What season is depicted here?

Reflections, 1981; acrylic ink serigraph
Harrison believed that the sun symbolizes perfection, and the sun appears in many colours in his Yukon paintings. Dogs and ravens often feature in his work as well. What do you think these animals could symbolize?

For twenty-five years, the Harrison family called the Yukon home. Ted's art became associated with Canada's northern skies and landscape. Ted's paintings evolved, showing northern houses, people and animals—all in flowing lines and imaginative colours.

As much as Ted loved teaching, he made the decision to retire in 1981 so he could dedicate himself to painting full time.

Tundra Books, a well-known Canadian publisher, produced his first book for children, *Children of the Yukon*. It was followed by *The Blue Raven*, published by Macmillan, and *A Northern Alphabet* for Tundra. Now people around the world could enjoy his stories and illustrations. Shows sold out across Canada and his work increased in popularity. In many places, people lined up around the block and through the night, in hopes of buying a Harrison.

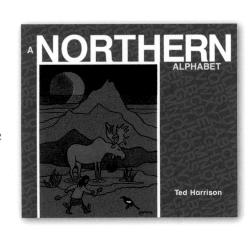

A Northern Alphabet,
book cover, 1982; acrylic
Harrison used his imagination when painting animals, people, skies and landscapes. Why do you think he chose a colour like pink for the moose?

Dog House, 1988; acrylic ink serigraph
Harrison had a special affection for animals, especially little dogs. The family owned a small black dog named Brunhilde, which can be found in many of his paintings.

Snowcat, 1987; acrylic ink serigraph
Note the unusual choice of orange, pink and red in this
painting. Blue outlining makes these colours work together
well, as do the black ravens.

The Boat, 1986; acrylic ink serigraph
This painting is filled with movement. What story does it tell?

In 1985, Kids Can Press asked Ted to illustrate the Robert Service poem "The Cremation of Sam McGee." Ted was thrilled at the chance to illustrate the words of the poet who had inspired him so many years before. Two years later, he illustrated another poem by Service, "The Shooting of Dan McGrew."

Ted designed the popular Yukon Pavilion for Expo '86 in Vancouver. People from all over the world admired his art as they walked "into" his painting to enter the Yukon exhibit.

One of Ted's most unusual designs includes the stained-glass windows in Christ Church Cathedral in Whitehorse, Yukon.

The Shooting of Dan McGrew, book cover image, 1987; acrylic
Harrison uses colour to contrast the warmth of the hotel interior with the chilly outdoor scene where the dog team waits. Does your eye travel around as you look at this painting, or do you focus on one section?

The Dr. Hilda Hellaby Window, 1987
This is one of two stained-glass windows that Harrison designed for Christ Church Cathedral in Whitehorse, Yukon. It was made by stained-glass artist Brenda Malkinson.

◀ *Expo '86 Yukon Pavilion*

Ted has become one of Canada's most beloved artists. His paintings hang in galleries and private collections throughout the world. In his own country, he has received many honours, including four honourary doctorate degrees. In 1987, he was awarded Canada's highest civilian honour, the Order of Canada. He was made a member of the Royal Canadian Academy of Arts in 2004 and was presented with the Order of British Columbia in 2008. Films and documentaries have been made about his life as an artist.

While many people of all ages love his bright, vivid colours and flowing lines, others laugh at his work, claiming it is so simple that even a child could do it. "What a compliment," Ted says. "Children know what is real, what is true." Even now, when Ted Harrison is considered one of Canada's most beloved painters, the National Gallery of Canada does not recognize his work.

"I am what I am," he likes to say. "Above all else, we must be who we are in everything we do, no matter what others say."

Skiers, 1988; acrylic ink serigraph
A playful raven joins skiers for a sunny day on the hills outside Carcross.

Sledding, 1989; acrylic ink serigraph
What clues tell us about the weather and time of day in this painting?
How does it differ from "Skiers"?

Ted and Nicky moved to Victoria, B.C., in 1993. They both missed the Yukon terribly. And at first, Ted, who was sixty-six, believed he might never paint again. The landscape was different; the light was different. But eventually, Ted captured the houses, the sea, the marine mammals and the fish boats of the West Coast.

Ted visited schools in Victoria and eventually travelled to schools across the country, telling stories and conducting art classes. He has never stopped thinking about education.

"Art must be part of every child's education," Ted Harrison says. "Painting is the last great freedom. You can paint what you like."

And so his legacy lives on, in the wisdom of his words, in the memories of his many students, in his books for children and in the joy his paintings continue to bring to people everywhere.

Mount Baker, 1993; acrylic ink serigraph
Compare the sky in this image of southern British Columbia with Harrison's depiction of the sky in his Yukon paintings.

Storm Flight, 1994; acrylic ink serigraph
Bright pink salmon dive deep as a storm brews above.

Acknowledgements

The authors wish to thank Ted Harrison, Charles Harrison and Barry Bergh for their enthusiasm, cooperation and assistance. Thank you to Gail Winskill and the whole team at Pajama Press for their unwavering enthusiasm.

Library Day, 1990; acrylic ink serigraph
Harrison told stories in his paintings and in the books he wrote. What might the child in the pink dress be saying to her father? Why is the dog wearing a saddle bag?

Sources & Resources

Books

A Northland Alphabet, Ted Harrison with Dr. W. D. Knill. Edmonton: University of Alberta Press, 1968

Children of the Yukon, Ted Harrison. Montreal: Tundra Books, 1977

The Last Horizon, Ted Harrison. Toronto: Merritt Publishing, 1980

A Northern Alphabet, Ted Harrison. Montreal: Tundra Books, 1982

The Blue Raven, Ted Harrison. Toronto: Macmillan of Canada, 1989

The Cremation of Sam McGee, Robert Service; illustrated by Ted Harrison. Toronto: Kids Can Press, 1986

The Shooting of Dan McGrew, Robert Service; illustrated by Ted Harrison. Toronto: Kids Can Press, 1988

O Canada, Poems by Sir Adolphe-Basile Routhier; commentary and illustrations by Ted Harrison. Toronto: Kids Can Press, 1992

Books About Ted Harrison

Ted Harrison: Painting Paradise, by Katherine Gibson, 2009
  www.katherinegibson.com

Websites

A fine collection of serigraphs for sale can be found at: **http://tedharrison.com/**

Ted's legacy to Canadian artists includes the Ted Harrison Artist residency program in Crag Lake, Yukon, where artists come together to work and study. More information can be found at: **www.tedharrisoncabin.com**

Films

Harrison's Yukon, National Film Board of Canada, 1979, 22 min 30 s

Land of the Chartreuse Moose: The Life and Legacy of Ted Harrison, Out Yonder Productions, 2011, 52 min

The Vet, 1991; acrylic ink serigraph

How do the blue sky and orange moon contrast with the activity in the lower part of this painting?

Index

Yukon Visit, 1990; acrylic ink serigraph
Whimsical, dancing skies dotted with snowflakes set the background
for a busy Yukon scene.